BABY ANIMALS
2

Published by Creative Education, Inc., 123 South Broad Street, Mankato, Minnesota 56001

Printed by permission of Wildlife Education, Ltd.

Library of Congress Cataloging-in-Publication Data

Elwood, Ann.
Baby Animals II / Ann Elwood.
p.   cm.
Summary: Describes the development and behavior of a variety of baby animals, including birds, reptiles, and mammals.
ISBN 0-88682-418-4
1. Animals—Infancy—Juvenile literature. [1. Animals—Infancy.] I. Title. II. Title: Baby animals 2. III. Title: Baby animals two.
QL763.E49   1991   591.3'9—dc20   91-7198 CIP AC

BABY ANIMALS
2

Series Created by
John Bonnett Wexo

Written by
Ann Elwood

Zoological Consultant
Charles R. Schroeder, D.V.M.
Director Emeritus
San Diego Zoo &
San Diego Wild Animal Park

Scientific Consultant
Charles Radcliffe, Ph.D.
Zoological Society of San Diego

Creative Education

Art Credits

Main Art: John Francis. **Page Eight: Top,** Walter Stuart; **Middle,** Walter Stuart; **Page Ten: Left,** Walter Stuart; **Page Nineteen: Middle Right,** Courtland L. Bovee. **Activities art** by Bonnie Pilson Kuhn.

Photographic Credits

Front Cover: Bill Losh (FPG International); **Pages Six and Seven:** Ray Richardson (Animals Animals); **Page Eight: Middle Left,** Paul Slick; **Middle,** Stephen Dalton (Natural History Photographic Agency); **Page Ten: Upper Middle,** Bob and Clara Calhoun (Bruce Coleman, Inc.); **Upper Right,** Veronica Tagland (Wildlife Education, Ltd.); **Page Eleven: Upper Right,** Hal H. Harrison (Grant Heilman Photography); **Pages Fourteen and Fifteen:** © Frans Lanting (Minden Pictures); **Page Sixteen: Lower Right,** Jack Dermid (Bruce Coleman, Inc.); **Page Seventeen: Middle Right,** Wolfgang Bayer (Bruce Coleman, Inc.); **Lower Left,** John Cancalosi (Tom Stack & Associates); **Page Eighteen: Left,** © S. Nielsen (DRK Photo); **Page Nineteen:** A.N.T. (Natural History Photographic Agency); **Page Twenty-one: Lower Middle,** Stephen J. Krasemann (Peter Arnold, Inc.); **Pages Twenty-two and Twenty-three:** All Photos by Veronica Tagland (Wildlife Education, Ltd.).

Our Thanks To: Dr. Virginia Landau and Dr. Judy Johnson (Jane Goodall Institute); Lisa Peters; Conor Mongan; Sean Mongan; Mike Mongan; Joe Selig.

Contents

Baby animals are magical—they grow and change into adults in fantastic ways. A downy chick becomes a smooth-feathered rooster, and a red comb sprouts on its head. A tadpole grows legs and turns into a frog. A fuzzy brown-and-white zebra becomes a sleek black-and-white adult.

Often baby animals look quite different than their parents. But what makes them look different is also what helps them stay alive during the first few weeks of their lives. The fuzzy yellow down on a chick helps to keep its small body warm. The long legs of a baby antelope help it run fast enough to keep up with the herd. If it couldn't keep up with the herd, it would quickly be eaten by predators.

When babies are not yet ready to take care of themselves, their parents will usually do the job. And sometimes, without thinking about it, babies do things that prod their parents into caring for them. When human babies cry, their parents feed them. The cheeping of a baby alligator causes its mother to help it break out of its shell. So even baby animals that *seem* very helpless have ways of staying alive.

But not all babies need parents to care for them. Most baby snakes never even know their mother. They can take care of themselves from the minute they are born. And they are good at defending themselves. For example, the poison in a baby rattlesnake's fangs is, drop for drop, more deadly than its parents' poison. So its bite can easily stop a predator that attacks it.

To survive, young animals sometimes have to learn very quickly. They usually learn faster than their parents. Like human children, animal babies learn serious lessons by playing. Lion cubs wrestle with each other, growling and tumbling over the ground, in what looks like a game. But they are actually practicing hunting skills and learning how to get along with each other. When baby horses run fast and kick up their heels, they are gaining skills for running with the herd to escape predators. When baby goats play "king of the mountain," they are actually learning to look out for predators from a high place. All in all, being a baby or young animal is one long lesson in *how to survive*.

Baby bighorn sheep

The starting point for almost all baby animals is the joining of a cell from the father and a cell from the mother to make a new cell. The new cell is so tiny that you cannot see it except under a microscope. Yet it will grow into a baby that is something like the mother and something like the father—but mostly like itself.

The helpless unborn baby, or *embryo* (em-BREE-oh), needs to grow inside a very safe, warm place. And it needs food, water, and oxygen (OX-ih-jen), which is a part of air. Some embryos develop inside an egg their mother lays. Others grow inside their mother's body.

These pictures show how a chicken embryo grows inside an egg. Once the two parent cells join, the new cell starts dividing into more cells.

Eggs laid on land have hard shells, which hold in the water that the embryo needs in order to live. The shell also protects the embryo from danger, and lets in air so that it can "breathe."

At 7 days, the embryo is mostly head and eyes. Tiny limbs are just beginning to form. But it's too soon to tell what kind of animal it will be.

Eggs laid in water won't dry out, so they don't need thick shells. Some eggs are so transparent that you can actually see the growing embryos inside. Can you see the tiny tadpoles inside these frog eggs?

At 21 days, the embryo has grown feathers. There are toenails on its scaly claws. Blood vessels carry food, oxygen, and water from the yolk and the rest of the egg to the embryo so that it can grow.

A mother sea turtle lays many eggs inside a hole she digs. Then she covers the eggs up with sand and goes away. Inside the eggs, the babies grow.

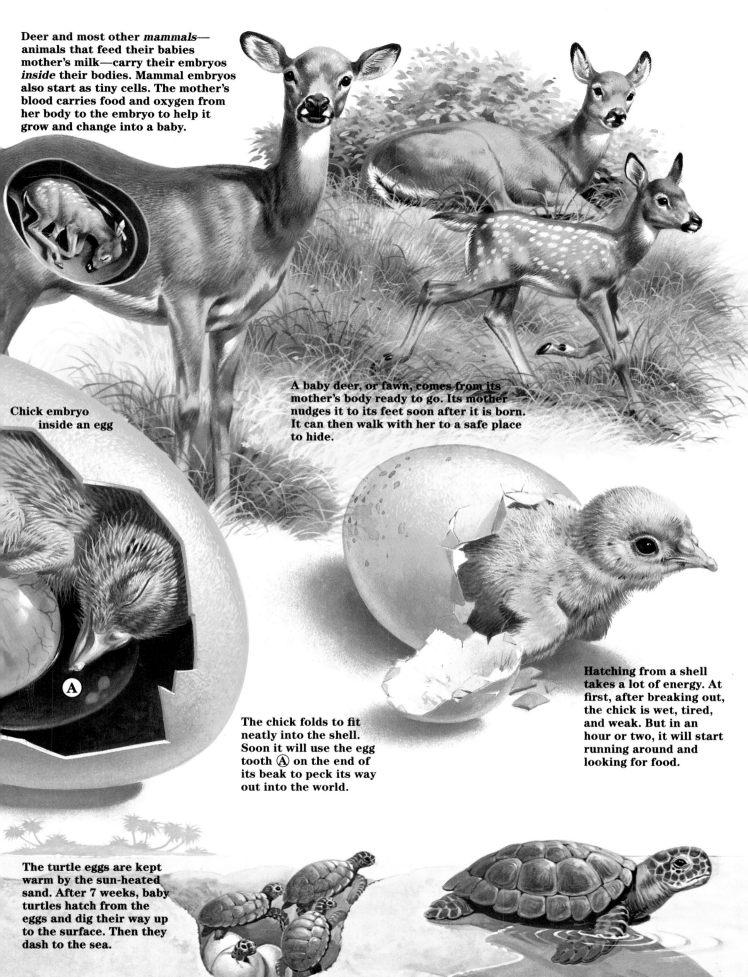

Deer and most other *mammals*—animals that feed their babies mother's milk—carry their embryos *inside* their bodies. Mammal embryos also start as tiny cells. The mother's blood carries food and oxygen from her body to the embryo to help it grow and change into a baby.

Chick embryo inside an egg

A baby deer, or fawn, comes from its mother's body ready to go. Its mother nudges it to its feet soon after it is born. It can then walk with her to a safe place to hide.

The chick folds to fit neatly into the shell. Soon it will use the egg tooth Ⓐ on the end of its beak to peck its way out into the world.

Hatching from a shell takes a lot of energy. At first, after breaking out, the chick is wet, tired, and weak. But in an hour or two, it will start running around and looking for food.

The turtle eggs are kept warm by the sun-heated sand. After 7 weeks, baby turtles hatch from the eggs and dig their way up to the surface. Then they dash to the sea.

Once born or hatched, many baby animals are able to follow their parents right away, though they may still need to be protected. These animals are called *precocial* (pre-KOH-shul). Other baby animals are born naked and helpless, not yet ready to take care of themselves at all. They are called *altricial* (al-TRISH-ul). The parents of altricial babies (and some precocial babies) often create shelters to keep the young ones safe and warm. Human mothers and fathers make cradles for their babies. Animals build nests, or they make holes in trees or burrows in the ground. Babies usually stay behind in the safe shelter while the parents search for food.

Some hummingbird nests are *no bigger than a quarter!* Tiny hummingbird babies are ready to fly 3 weeks after they are hatched.

Actual size

Raccoons and squirrels often have their babies in holes in trees. Sometimes they make nests in the holes. The babies are safe from predators like the fox that cannot climb trees.

ASIA

NORTH AMERICA

Gray whales don't make shelters. But in summer they *migrate* (travel) thousands of miles south to warm bays to have their babies. Their calves can grow faster there because they don't waste energy fighting the cold.

South American ovenbirds mold mud lumps into a nest like a little house. The mother bird lays her eggs and raises the babies in a grass-lined room inside. In summer, when the nest gets so hot it is like a real oven, the young birds leave.

When altricial birds hatch, they cannot stand or see. Because they have no feathers, their parents have to keep them warm. And if the sun beats down on altricial babies, they might even sunburn!

Precocial wood ducks jump out of the nest and flop to the ground right after hatching. They have strong legs and a layer of down to keep them warm. Even though they can swim, they cannot fly and need their parents to protect them and help them find food.

Within less than an hour after birth, zebra babies can stand and run. If they could not run right away, a predator might eat them!

A small bird called the American verdin builds a thorn nest lined with grass that looks like a porcupine. Sometimes the nest sits in a thorn bush. Predators who try to grab baby verdins can be stabbed.

Tiny baby rabbits, which are altricial, are born 3 to 6 at a time in an underground burrow. Their mother lines the burrow with grass and her own fur. When she leaves the burrow to find food, she hides the entrance with dirt or grass to keep the babies safe and warm.

*A*nimal babies are born and grow up in families of all sizes and kinds. Certain kinds of families are small—like a mother and father bird and their nestlings. Others are huge—some kinds of fish have hundreds of babies.

When babies grow old enough to leave the nest or den, they often join a larger family of relatives. For instance, a big family of females—mothers, sisters, and aunts—may live together and share child care. The males may live apart from the group, but they still help to protect the females and babies from predators.

A mother elephant takes very good care of her baby. If a lion comes too near, she trumpets a loud warning sound and then charges at top speed. Sometimes the calf charges right along with her!

Born in deep winter, a tiny newborn polar bear only weighs about a pound (450 grams). It lives in a snow cave with its huge mother and another cub. After the family leaves the cave in the spring, it stays together for another year.

The Great Indian hornbill male brings food to his mate and their nestlings, who are safely walled with mud inside a tree. He may make as many as 70 feeding trips a day for several weeks. When the babies are ready to take care of themselves, they come out of the hole.

Some babies are on their own from birth. Many kinds of snakes hatch out of their eggs ready to deal with the world. They never know their parents at all.

Wolves live in packs of males and females. But for the first 3 weeks after their birth in the spring, wolf cubs stay with their mother in a den apart from the rest. They live on mother's milk.

Soon, the cub joins the larger group of wolves and begins to explore the outside world. By chasing frogs together, young wolves learn to hunt in a pack. But the den is still home.

When cubs are 3 months old, they join hunting parties. By fall, they don't need to depend on their parents any more. But most still live with the pack.

13

Black-browed albatross chicks

Many kinds of animals carry their babies to keep them safe from danger. If an enemy comes too near, they pick up their babies and run. Some animals even take their babies with them when they search for food. Carrying babies can be very handy. A parent can move from place to place without having to worry about the baby or remember its hiding place. But an animal needs some way of carrying the baby—hands, a mouth, or even a pouch. And the baby usually has to be very good at holding on tight.

Baby bats cling to their mothers as they fly. When they get too heavy to carry, their mother hangs them up in the bat roost while she hunts for food.

Tiny baby opposums are usually born in big litters. Like all *marsupials*, they spend their first few months in their mother's pouch. When they get too big for the pouch, they ride on her back, sometimes 12 to 14 at a time!

Sea otter babies are born ashore. But they soon go to sea, riding on their mothers' stomachs. The mothers groom and feed the babies as they float along.

A baby chimpanzee rides on its mother's body, holding on to her hair. Like a human baby, it can grip tightly with its fingers. When it is very young, it usually clings to its mother's chest. Later on, it rides like a jockey on her back.

Swans and other water birds let their babies ride on their backs. High above the water, they are safe from big fish that like to eat baby birds. And their parents' feathers keep them warm.

Crocodile babies hatch in batches of 40 to 50. Their mother then picks them up in her mouth, about 6 at a time, and carries them from the nest to a safe nursery pool.

When scorpion babies are born, their mother carries them on her back, as many as a dozen at a time. Any animal that tries to eat the babies will get a surprise from the mother's big stinger!

Kangaroos also carry their babies in body pouches. When the young kangaroos, or *joeys*, grow big, they climb out of the pouch to see the world. But when there is danger, they jump back in again.

All babies are born knowing how to do certain things. For instance, snakes will crawl whether or not they ever see anybody else do it. So will human babies. Some babies, especially those that are on their own from birth, are born with *everything* they need to know in order to behave like other animals of their kind. This inborn sense is called *instinct* (IN-stinkt).

Imprinting is a special kind of instinct. One type of imprinting makes babies follow the first thing they see. This helps to keep them safe, because, like an invisible leash, it keeps them close to their watchful parents, even when they are on the move.

Some young animals—especially those that live in groups—must *learn* how to do things by watching other animals of their kind. And even animals that are born knowing how to do certain things still need practice to do them right.

Mother swans defend their babies ferociously. Because baby swans are imprinted to their mother, they always stay close to her, even when she is fighting off a predator.

Right after hatching, young ducklings follow the *first thing they see moving.* And they *keep* following it for weeks. Usually what they see is their mother. Yet ducklings might follow a boy on a tricycle if he turned out to be the first thing they saw.

When traveling, a shrew family forms a chain, like kids in line holding hands, with the mother in the lead. Each baby knows instinctively that it must hold on to the shrew in front of it. This keeps them all close to their mother so that she can protect them.

A baby skunk is born knowing how to spray an enemy. This protects it from predators, like this fox, even when no adult is around. No animal, even the skunk, likes strong skunk spray!

Most birds sing a song that is special to their kind. Through *instinct*, baby birds can sing a rough form of that song without ever hearing it sung by another bird. But to sing the *full* song, babies need to hear and copy adults—to *learn* it.

Baby birds tell their parents when they are hungry by simply opening their brightly colored mouths! This behavior is called "gaping."

The herring gull chick does more than gape. When it is hungry, it pecks at a red spot at the base of its parent's bill to make the parent feed it.

When young animals play, they develop muscles and skills for survival. Some young animals play at make-believe hunting or fighting. And they usually have ways of showing that they are pretending and won't really hurt each other. Young "hunters" learn to figure out how far away danger is, how to time an attack, and how to surprise an enemy. If you have ever watched kittens playing, you have seen this in action.

But hunting and fighting are not all that young animals learn through playing. They also practice escaping from predators. They learn to get along with each other. And they learn the signals of their group—like the signal for danger.

When chimps play at fighting, they wear a special "play face" to show each other that they mean no harm.

PLAY FACE

An angry chimp wears a "threat face" to show that it means business.

When rhesus monkeys want to play, they look at each other upside down through their legs.

THREAT FACE

Baby rhesus monkeys love to chase each other through the trees. By swinging after each other on the vines, they practice keeping up with the group. And they develop strong muscles for escaping from predators.

Baby bears are smaller than adult bears, so they can climb higher into trees without the branches breaking. But it doesn't matter that adult bears can't climb so high. They are strong enough to defend themselves on the ground.

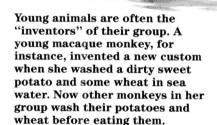

Young animals are often the "inventors" of their group. A young macaque monkey, for instance, invented a new custom when she washed a dirty sweet potato and some wheat in sea water. Now other monkeys in her group wash their potatoes and wheat before eating them.

Baby dolphins play in the sea waves. Sometimes they chase each other in rough-and-tumble games of tag or keep-away. This is how they sharpen their skills in catching food.

Chimpanzees are curious animals, just like human children. One way they show their curiosity is by punching holes in leaves and looking through them.

Baby Animals Activities

Be a good egg, take a crack at the baby animals activities on these two pages. Use what you have learned about baby animals to complete these fun exercises.

Tiger

AlphaBabies

It's as easy as ABC. Write your name using AlphaBabies instead of regular letters. Design your own AlphaBabies. If you wish, use the ones shown above as models. Try this word right away.

B A B Y

Are You My Mother?

Match each baby animal to its mother.

Baby Fingers

Make an animal baby finger puppet. Then make your puppet run and play.

You will need: scraps of fabric or felt, scissors, needle and thread, white glue.

1. Cut out two pieces of fabric or felt to match the shape of the pattern. Sew the two pieces together. Follow the stitch marks shown on the pattern.
2. Design your animal baby's face. You might make sketches on paper. Cut out pieces of fabric or felt. Glue the pieces together to make your puppet.

Pattern
CUT 2

Stitches

Raccoon

Panda

You've Got the Cutest Little Baby Face

Go ahead, make a face. Use make-up, colored zinc oxide, or face paint to recreate one of these baby faces. Or be even more creative and "make up" a baby face of your own.

A Kitten by Any Other Name . . .

As you know, a baby cat is called a kitten and a baby dog is called a puppy or pup. But did you know that a baby beaver is also called a pup? Can you guess to what animal parent a shoat belongs? (The answer is to a hog.) More strange animal baby names are shown below. How many of them do you recognize? Find one or more adult names for each of the baby names shown. You can use a dictionary for help.

calf	fawn	kid
chick	fledgling	kit
cub	gosling	poult
cygnet	joey	whelp

Answers

3. scales   6. caterpillar
2. wings   5. silk button
1. eggs   4. antennae

Read More About Baby Animals

How Animals Care for Their Babies by Roger B. Hirschland. Washington, D.C.: National Geographic Society, 1987.

Discover some of the many different ways in which animal families take care of their young. And learn about babies that take care of themselves! Beautiful photographs make this book hard to put down.

Chickens Aren't the Only Ones by Ruth Heller. New York: Grosset and Dunlap, 1981.

For readers who think that chickens are the only animals that lay eggs, this book is full of surprises. Beautiful illustrations and poetic words make this award-winning picture book egg-ceptional.

It's a Jungle Out There

There's a jungle in Pat's backyard. Can you see what Pat sees? Can you find the cat, deer, mouse, raccoon, squirrel, frog, and chicken in Pat's garden?

Index